# A Frog's Dangerous Home

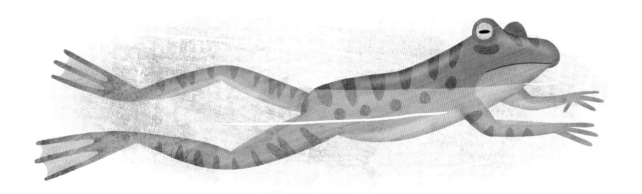

by Mary Ellen Klukow

Illustrated by Romina Martí

## About the Author

After earning her B.S. in Wildlife and Conservation Biology from Ohio University, Mary Ellen Klukow spent the first few years of her career in environmental research. She is now proud and happy to share her knowledge with young readers.

## About the Illustrator

Romina Martí is an illustrator who lives and works in Barcelona, Spain, where her ideas come to life for all audiences. She loves to discover and draw all kinds of creatures from around the planet, who then become the main characters for the majority of her work. To learn more, go to rominamarti.com

AMICUS ILLUSTRATED is published by Amicus and Amicus Ink.
P.O. Box 1329, Mankato, MN 56002
www.amicuspublishing.us

LIBRARY OF CONGRESS CATALOGING-IN-PUBLICATION DATA
Names: Klukow, Mary Ellen, author. | Martí, Romina, illustrator.
Title: A frog's dangerous home / by Mary Ellen Klukow ; illustrated by Romina Martí.
Description: Mankato, Minnesota : Amicus/Amicus Ink, [2020] |
Series: Animal habitats at risk | Audience: K to grade 3.
Identifiers: LCCN 2018051671 (print) | LCCN 2018055695 (ebook) | ISBN 9781681517834 (pdf) | ISBN 9781681517018 (library binding) | ISBN 9781681524870 (pbk.)
Subjects: LCSH: Mountain yellow-legged frog—Juvenile literature. | Frogs—Habitat—Juvenile literature. | Habitat conservation—Juvenile literature. | Rare amphibians—Conservation—Juvenile literature.
Classification: LCC QL668.E27 (ebook) | LCC QL668. E27 K58 2020 (print) | DDC 333.95/789—dc23
LC record available at https://lccn.loc.gov/2018051671

EDITOR: Wendy Dieker
DESIGNER: Kathleen Petelinsek

Printed in the United States of America
HC 10 9 8 7 6 5 4 3 2 1
PB 10 9 8 7 6 5 4 3 2 1

*Click. Click.* Did you hear that? That was the croak of a mountain yellow-legged frog. He calls for a mate.

This frog was hibernating on the bottom of a lake. He lives high in the California mountains. It wasn't too long ago when frogs were dying in this lake. A deadly fungus was killing them.

Now this frog is awake and ready to mate. First, he must eat. A bright blue dragonfly flies by.

The frog's sticky tongue darts out of his mouth. It grabs the
bug! Gulp! In the blink of an eye, the dragonfly is gone.

Frogs eat all kinds of bugs. They help keep bugs from becoming a problem. But if there aren't many bugs, frogs won't have enough food.

The frog sees two scientists on the shore.
They are here to test the water. One scientist
collects a water sample to check for pesticides.

Pesticides are chemicals that kill plants and bugs. The frog's skin absorbs air and water. If there are chemicals in the water, the frogs in the lake will get sick.

Suddenly a net falls over the frog! A scientist picks him up. She softly runs a cotton swab across his skin. She is checking for chytrid fungus. Chytrid fungus kills amphibians all over the world. The scientists hope this frog doesn't have the fungus.

The scientist gently returns the frog to the ground. She didn't hurt the frog, and he is ready to continue searching for his mate.

He jumps back into the water and starts swimming away.

Whoosh! Suddenly, the frog realizes he's being chased! A trout races up with its mouth open wide. It is trying to eat the frog! The frog kicks his strong legs and swims under a log. He is safe for now.

These trout weren't always in this lake. They are invasive.
They were stocked in this lake so people could go fishing.

16

The frogs are not used to the trout. Some of them don't escape. There are fewer frogs in the lake.

17

The frog pops up. He sees two googly eyes staring back at him. It is a female mountain yellow-legged frog!

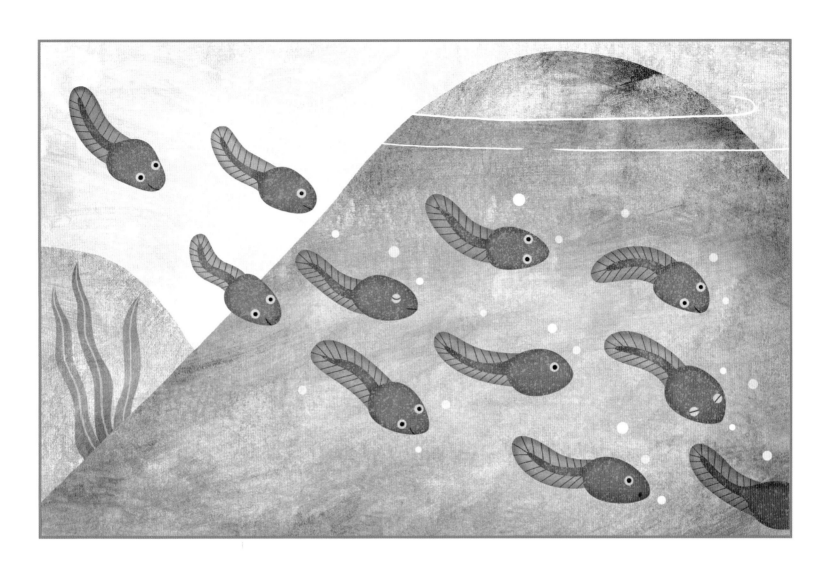

He has found a mate. After mating, the female will
lay up to 350 eggs. They will hatch into tadpoles.

This frog is lucky. Yellow-legged frogs nearly died out in this lake. But scientists have worked hard to help frogs fight the chytrid fungus in the lake. Now the number of frogs is growing. Frogs need us to help keep their homes clean and safe.

# Where Mountain Yellow-Legged Frogs Live

Mountain yellow-legged frogs live in alpine lakes along North America's West Coast.

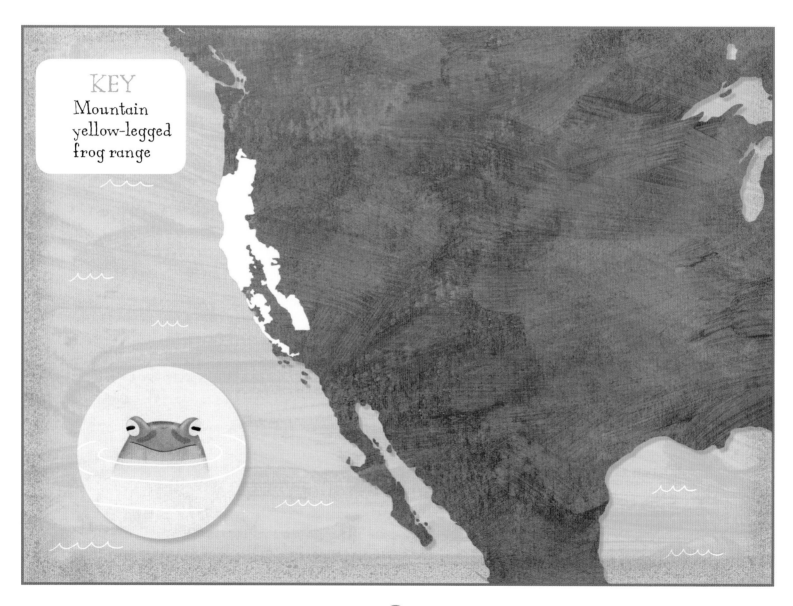

KEY
Mountain yellow-legged frog range

# Frogs at Risk

Frogs all over the world are facing danger. Invasive predators and water pollution are big problems for them. Luckily, natural resources departments and volunteer groups are helping. They remove pollution like trash from frog habitats, teach people how to avoid pesticides, and even take frogs to labs to help them fight chytrid fungus.

## You can help frogs!

- Buy organic food! Organic farmers don't use pesticides.
- Write letters! Ask government officials to write laws that help keep the environment safe for all animals.
- Build a backyard pond. Frogs and other amphibians everywhere need a clean and safe place to live.

# Glossary

**absorb** To soak up liquids or gasses through tiny holes in the skin called pores.

**invasive** A plant or animal that is not originally from an area and is causing problems.

**mate** One of two animals in a pair that comes together to make babies.

**pesticides** Chemicals meant to kill unwanted insects, animals, or plants.

**tadpole** A baby frog that just hatched from an egg; tadpoles go through a transformation to become frogs.

# Read More

Bath, Louella. *Saving Endangered Animals.* New York: PowerKids Press, 2017.

Bell, Samantha S. *12 Amphibians Back from the Brink.* North Mankato, Minn.: 12-Story Library, 2015.

Kelly, Irene. *A Frog's Life.* New York: Holiday House, 2018.

# Websites

Association of Zoos and Aquariums: Top 8 Ways to Help Frogs
*https://www.speakcdn.com/assets/2332 /top_8_ways_to_help_frogs.pdf*
Learn how to save frogs in your own backyard.

Ecology: Indicator Species and Proud of It
*http://www.ecology.com/2011/11/01 /indicator-species-proud/*
What is an indicator species? Why are frogs important? Find out here!

Can the Frog Apocalypse be Stopped by a New "Vaccine"? | Deep Look
*https://youtu.be/-IXVcyCZVBg*
Watch how scientists are working to save frogs.

Every effort has been made to ensure that these websites are appropriate for children. However, because of the nature of the Internet, it is impossible to guarantee that these sites will remain active indefinitely or that their contents will not be altered.